Harriet Tubman and Her Life

An Interactive Book
By Rich Linville
ISBN: 9781723794322

Around 1820, I am born into slavery in the state of Maryland with the name of Araminta Ross. My nickname is Minty. Maybe my name will change later.

As I become older, I change my name to honor my mother, Harriet. Can you find the state where I was born on a map of the United States?

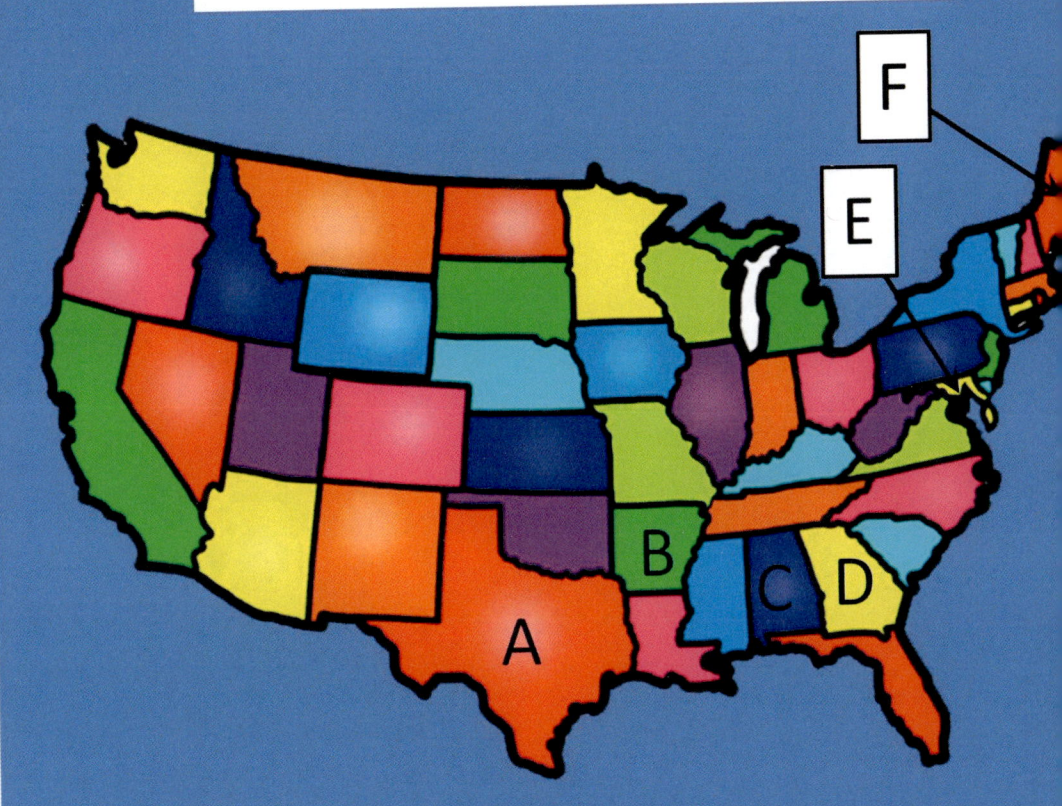

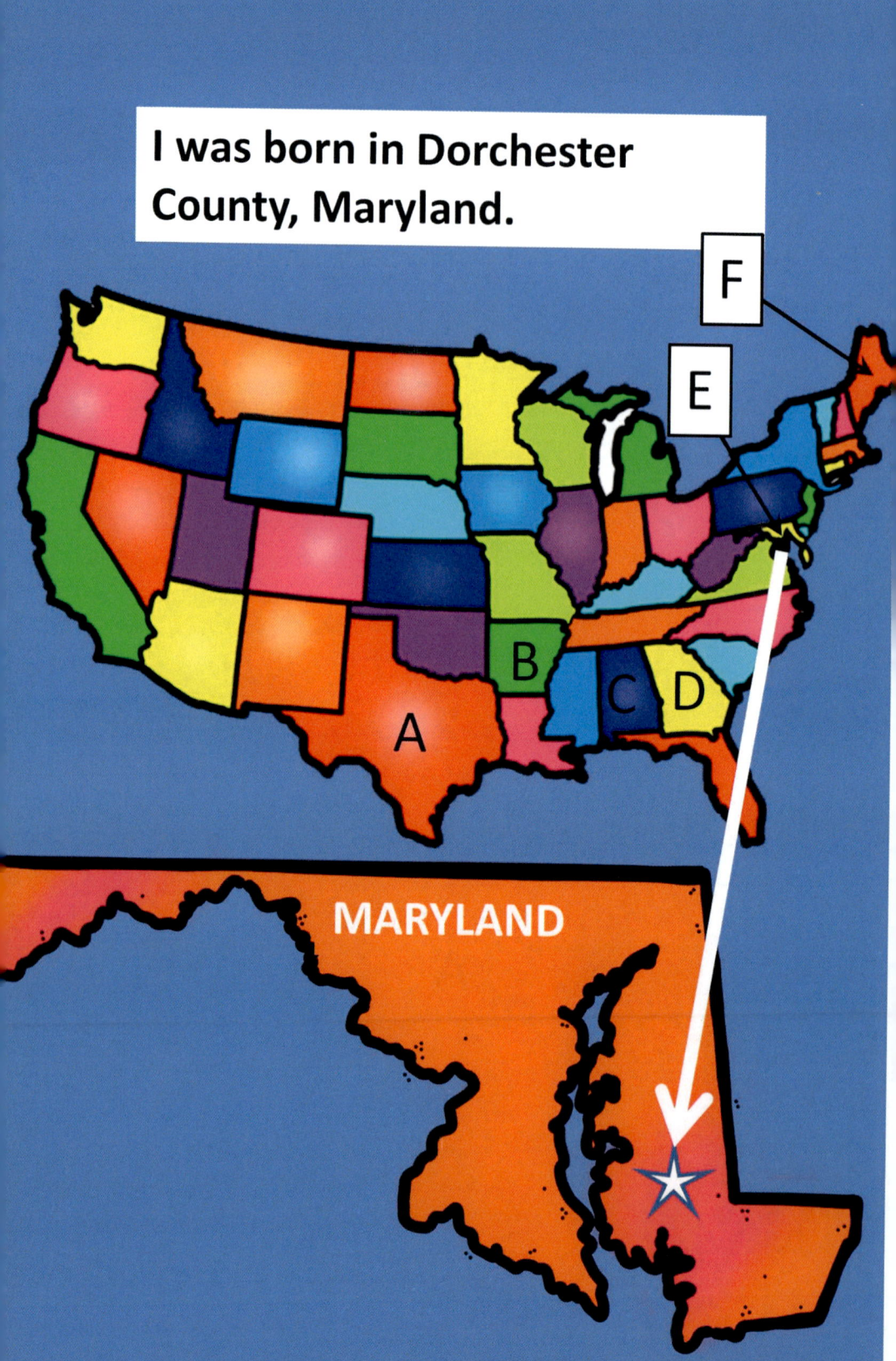

I'm twelve years old scarred and emotionally hurt. I am beaten and whipped by my slave owners if I make the smallest mistake. My head is hit by a heavy metal weight thrown by an angry master. I believe that my hair saves my life because it has never been combed and stands out like a basket.

Upon the death of my master in 1840, my family is set free in his will. But a new owner does not agree to the will and keeps us as slaves. I fear being sold to pick cotton in the South. Picking by hand is backbreaking work.

In 1849, with my brothers Ben and Henry, I escape from our Maryland plantation. My brothers decide to go back. Should I travel on the Underground Railroad?

The Underground Railroad is not a real railroad. It's many different secret pathways to the north to freedom. Runaway slaves will travel at night and stay at safe houses to hide during the day. The person who helps the slaves escape is called a Conductor.

In 1831, a slave called Tice Davids escaped from Kentucky to freedom in Ohio. The slave owner of Tice blamed the escape on an Underground Railroad. The name stuck. Do I go on the Underground Railroad to get my freedom?

I decide to follow the lip of the Big Dipper that points to the North Star in the handle of the Little Dipper.
I don't give up. Using the Underground Railroad, I walk 90 miles north to Pennsylvania and to freedom in just a few days.

In Philadelphia, Pennsylvania, I find a paid job as a housekeeper. But I want freedom for others who are enslaved.

I go back to Maryland, to help other slaves escape to freedom. Even though we travel at night, we have to watch out for bounty hunters who are paid thousands of dollars for returning slaves to their owners. Some bounty hunters carry guns and will shoot us if we run away.

I whisper, "Quiet! It's a bounty hunter. Let's go another way."
I see is a Wanted Poster with a description of me that offers a $40,000 reward to anyone capturing or else shooting me. Do I still help other slaves escape?

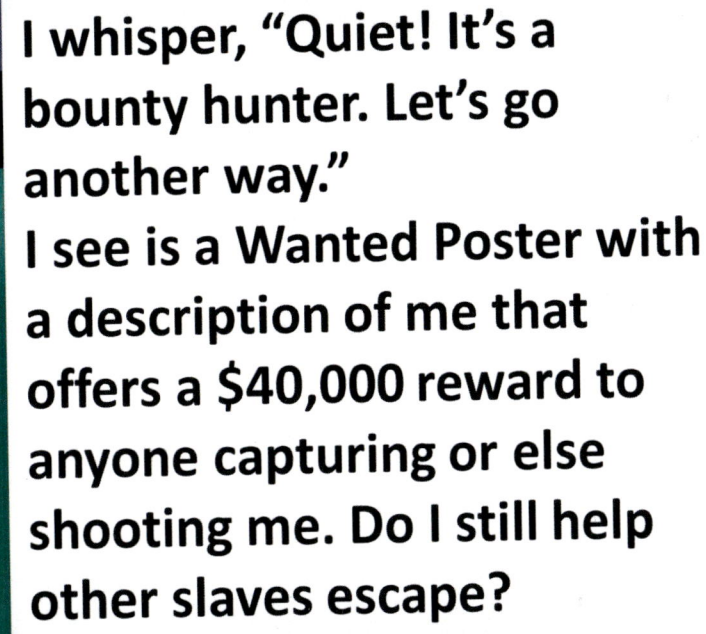

WANTED
DEAD OR ALIVE
For Stealing Slaves
Harriet "Moses" Tubman
$40,000 Reward

Negro slave about 5 feet tall, Scars on her neck and a deep scar on her forehead. Plain woman of short stature, upper front teeth missing, with a habit of abruptly falling asleep. Looks harmless but she carries a pistol.

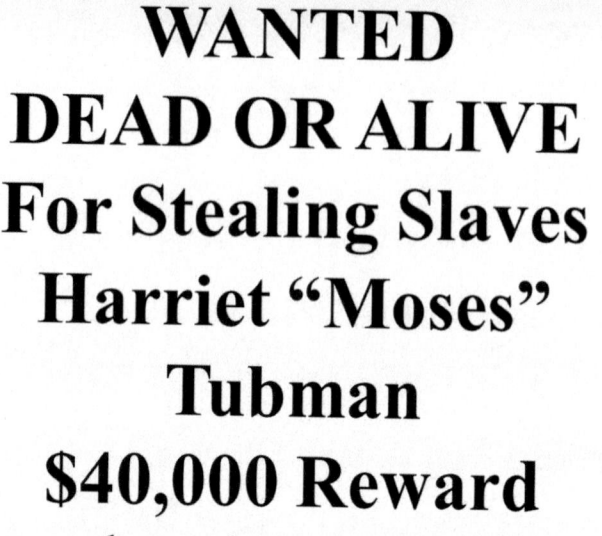

In 10-years time, as a conductor, I help over 300 slaves escape to the north and freedom. I've never lost a passenger. My nick name is "Moses," like the one who freed the slaves from the Egyptian Pharaoh. What will happen to our United States in 1861?

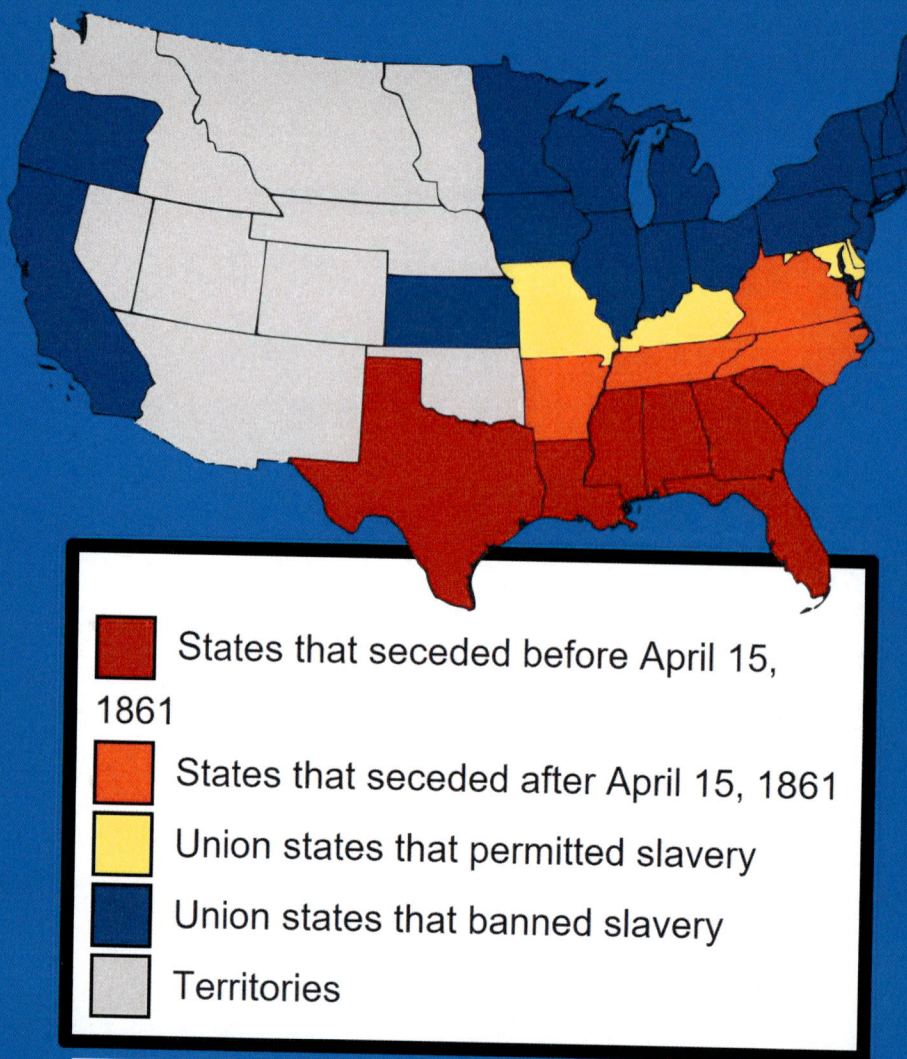

States that seceded before April 15, 1861

States that seceded after April 15, 1861

Union states that permitted slavery

Union states that banned slavery

Territories

The American Civil War begins in 1861 when some states leave the Union. I work for the Union Army as a cook and a nurse. Later, I become a scout and spy.

On January 1, 1863, President Abraham Lincoln frees the Southern slaves with the Emancipation Proclamation.

On June 2, 1863, my scouts and I learn of a large group of slaves being held near the Combahee River in South Carolina. I plan a nighttime raid and map the location of bombs in the river. On June 2nd, I safely guide three steam warships up the river.

We set fire to plantations, grab supplies and free more than 700 slaves. My Combahee River Raid was a huge success for the North and weakened the South. Many of the freed slaves went on to join the Black Union Army. What will I do after the Civil War ends?

After the Civil War ends in 1865, I retire to my family home in Auburn, New York, where I care for my aging parents.

I become active in the women's suffrage movement which says that women should have the same rights and pay for work as men do. Will I succeed?

I am active in the women's suffrage movement until illness overtakes me. I am admitted to a home for elderly African Americans that I had helped to establish. After I die in 1913, I become a symbol of American freedom and courage.

Map of Important Monuments of Harriet Tubman

For some slave owners, if slaves made mistakes, they are whipped by their masters. For how long, do you think slavery existed in the United States?

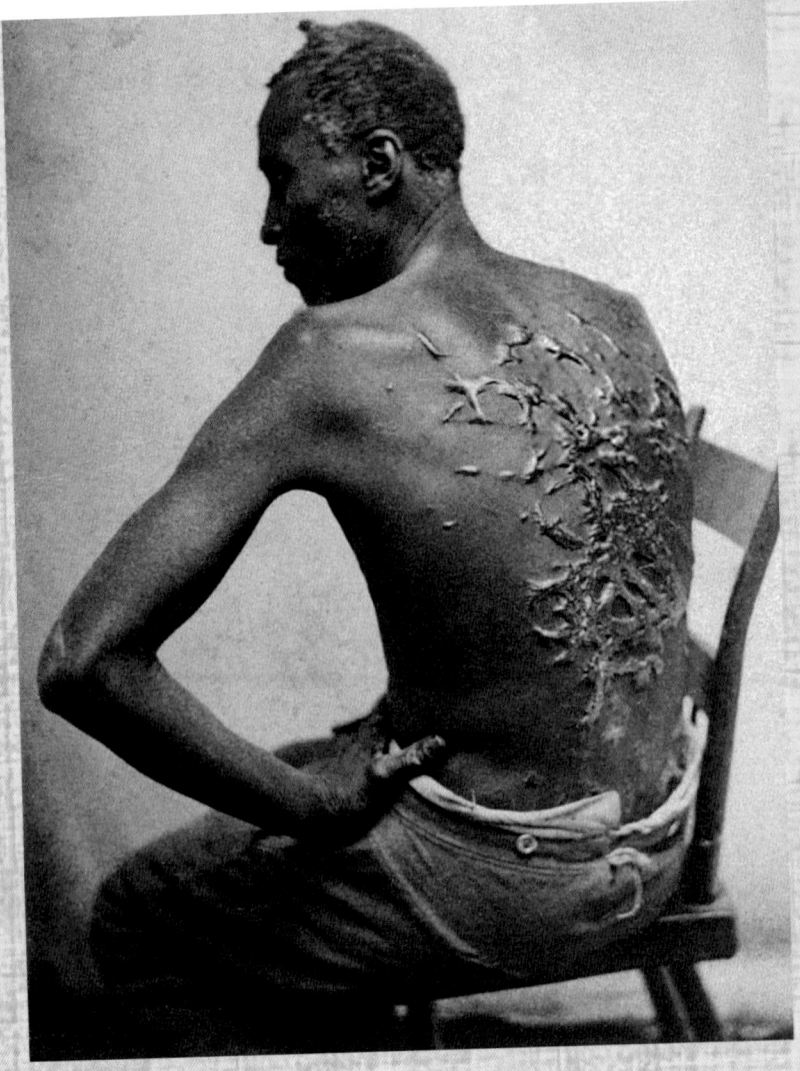

In the US, slavery started in 1619. Slaves were brought by ships across the Atlantic Ocean from Europe, Africa and the Caribbean Islands until 1865.

Quotes By Harriet Tubman

"Every great dream begins with a dreamer."
- Harriet Tubman

"If you hear the dogs, keep going. If you see the torches in the woods, keep going. If there's shouting after you, keep going. Don't ever stop. Keep going. If you want a taste of freedom, keep going." - Harriet Tubman

Quotes By Harriet Tubman

"I was the conductor of the Underground Railroad for eight years, and I can say what most conductors can't say; I never ran my train off the track and I never lost a passenger."
Harriet Tubman

Quotes By Harriet Tubman

"The Lord who told me to take care of my people meant me to do it just as long as I live, and so I did what he told me."
- Harriet Tubman

"Lord, I'm going to hold steady on to You and You've got to see me through."
- Harriet Tubman

Quotes By Harriet Tubman

"In my dreams and visions, I seemed to see a line, and on the other side of that line were green fields, and lovely flowers, and beautiful white ladies, who stretched out their arms to me over the line, but I couldn't reach them no-how. I always fell before I got to the line."- Harriet Tubman

"I had reasoned this out in my mind, there was one of two things I had a right to, liberty or death; if I could not have one, I would have the other". - Harriet Tubman

Dedicated to my lovely wife Sulastri and my grandchildren Mia and Kai as well as everyone who enjoys learning history.

For over 40 years, I have enjoyed teaching at elementary, high school and college levels.

I would love to hear from you. You can email me at richardvlinville@gmail.com

Please check out my other books at bookstores and online under the name Rich Linville.

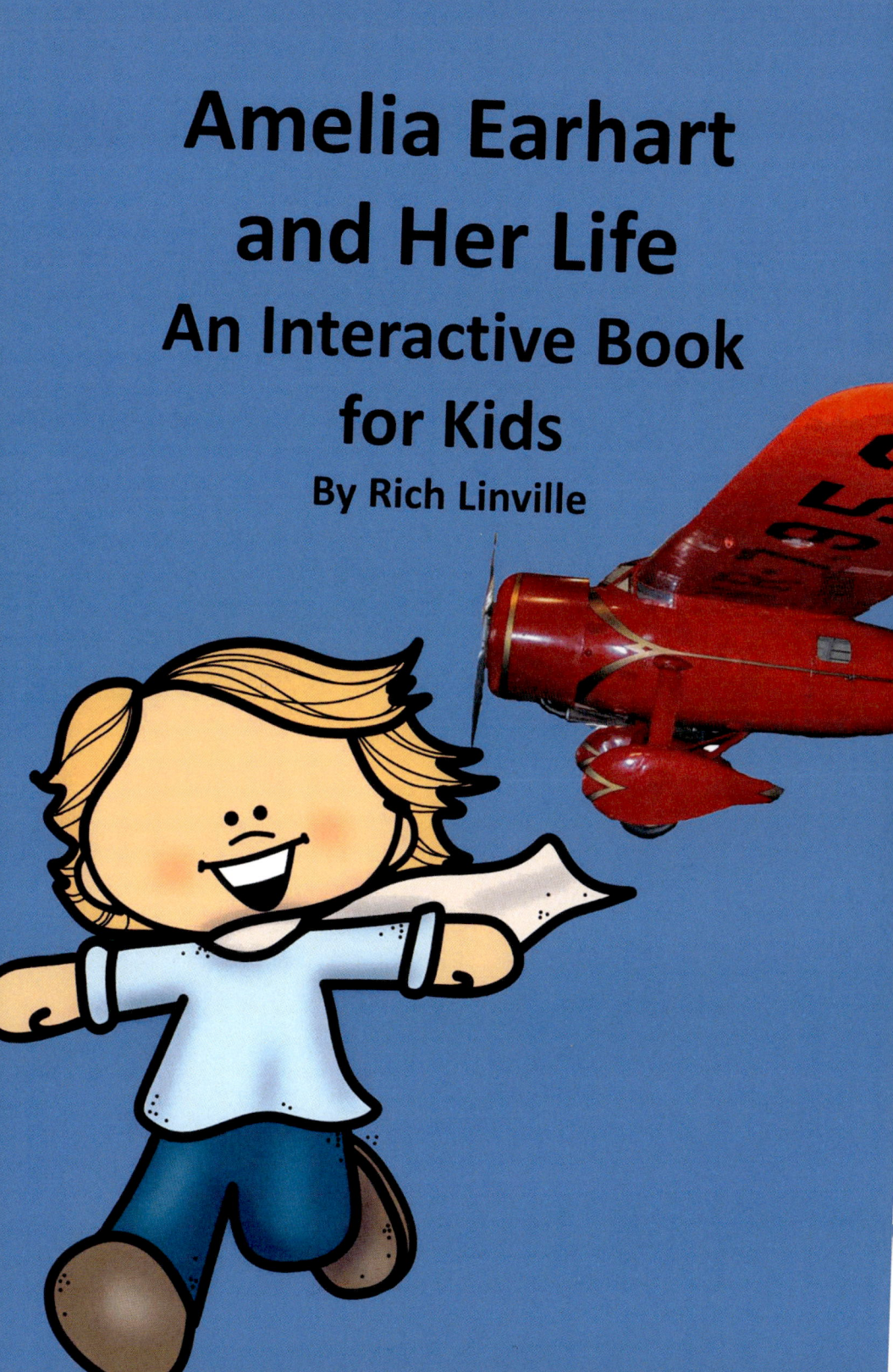

Amelia Earhart and Her Life
An Interactive Book for Kids
By Rich Linville

Unicorn Jokes for Kids and How to Tell Them

Written by Rich Linville

My Basketball Blues
from the Basketball's Point of View
Written by Rich Linville

My Rocky Adventure!
By Rocky Magma
Written by Rich Linville

Someday I'd like to be
a rock instead of magma

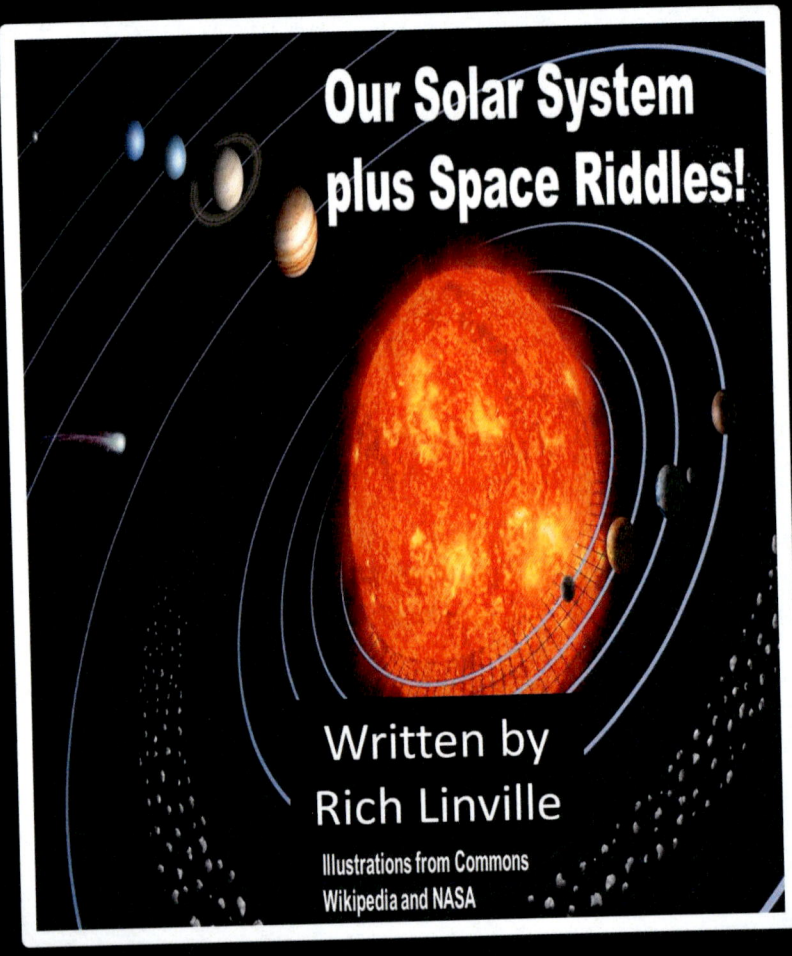

Actual photos of our sun, planets and a dwarf planet. Learn about our solar system with a trick to remember the order of the planets.

Illustrations from OpenClipArt, PixaBay, Commons Wiki and illustrations purchased from Edu-Clips.com.

Made in the USA
Coppell, TX
28 July 2023

19647232R10026